THANK YOU GOD!

By Hope Fields
Visuals by Jamie Hill

ELM HILL

A Division of
HarperCollins Christian Publishing

www.elmhillbooks.com

THANK YOU GOD!

Published in Nashville, Tennessee, by Elm Hill, an imprint of Thomas Nelson. Elm Hill and Thomas Nelson are registered trademarks of HarperCollins Christian Publishing, Inc.

Elm Hill titles may be purchased in bulk for educational, business, fund-raising, or sales promotional use. For information, please e-mail SpecialMarkets@ThomasNelson.com.

Library of Congress Cataloging-in-Publication Data

Library of Congress Control Number: 2018960002

ISBN 978-0-310102014 (Paperback)
ISBN 978-0-310102021 (Ebook)

THANK YOU GOD!

THANK YOU GOD
for heaven and earth.

Genesis 1:1-2

THANK YOU GOD
for making day and night.
We sleep in the dark…

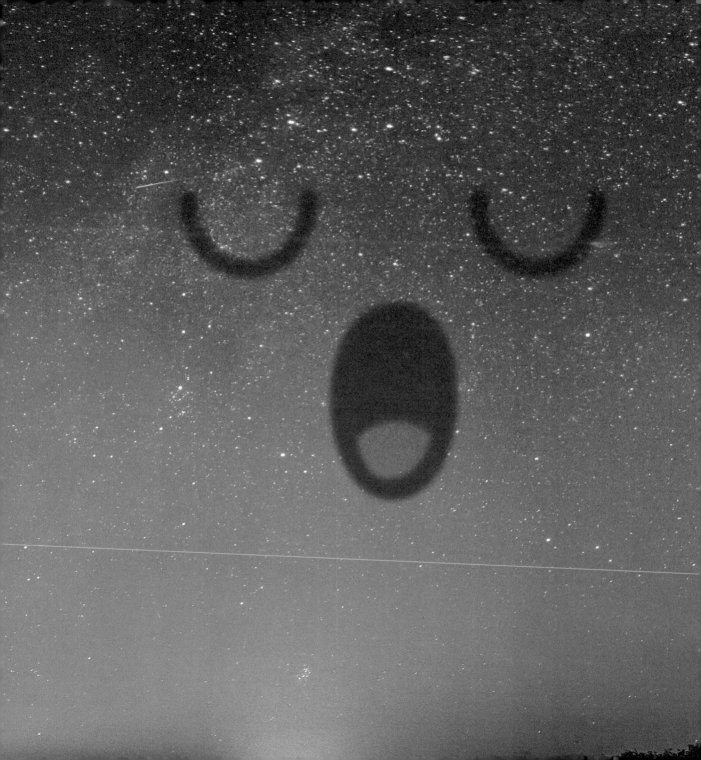

and AWAKE **in the light.**

Genesis 1: 3-8

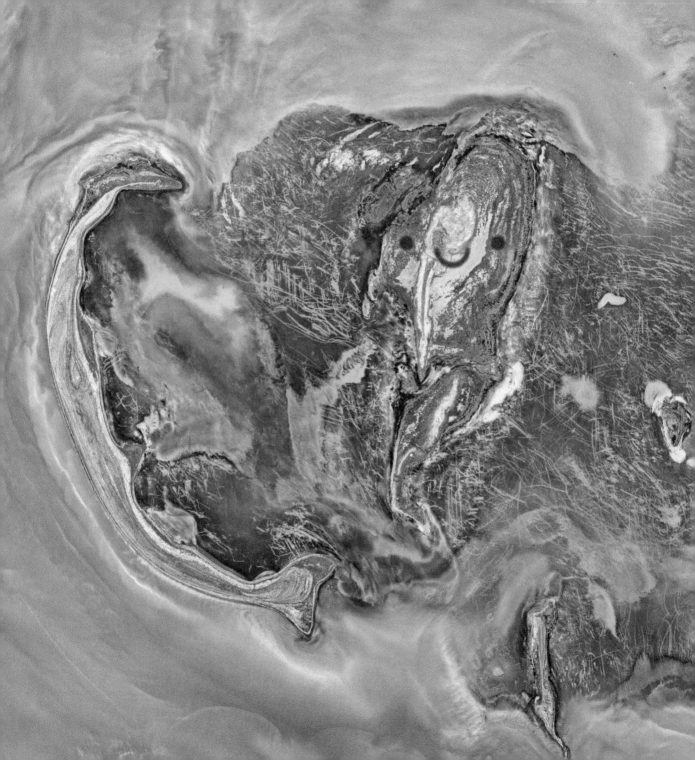

to plant seeds to GROW fruits and veggies.

Genesis 1: 9-13

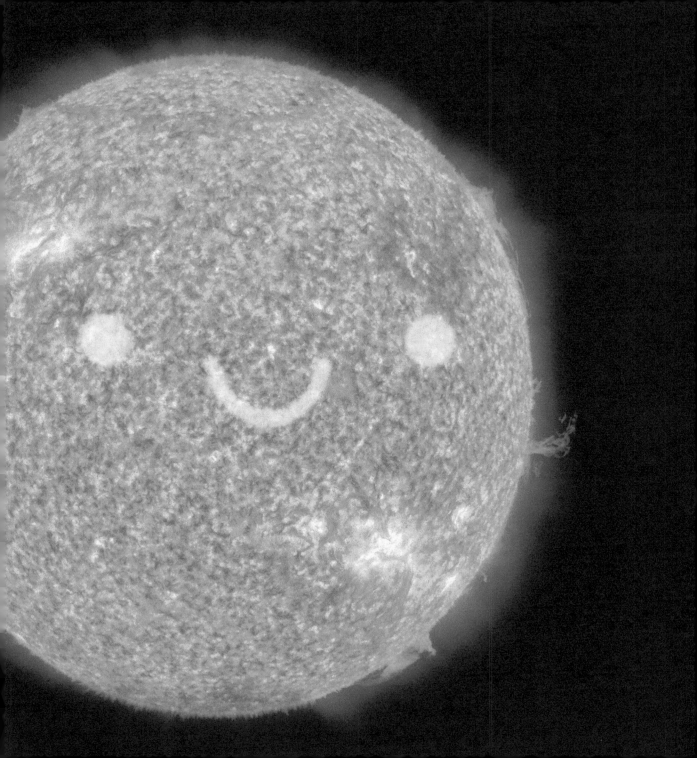

THANK YOU GOD
for the sun and moonlight.
One shines in the day and
one at night.

Genesis 1: 14-19

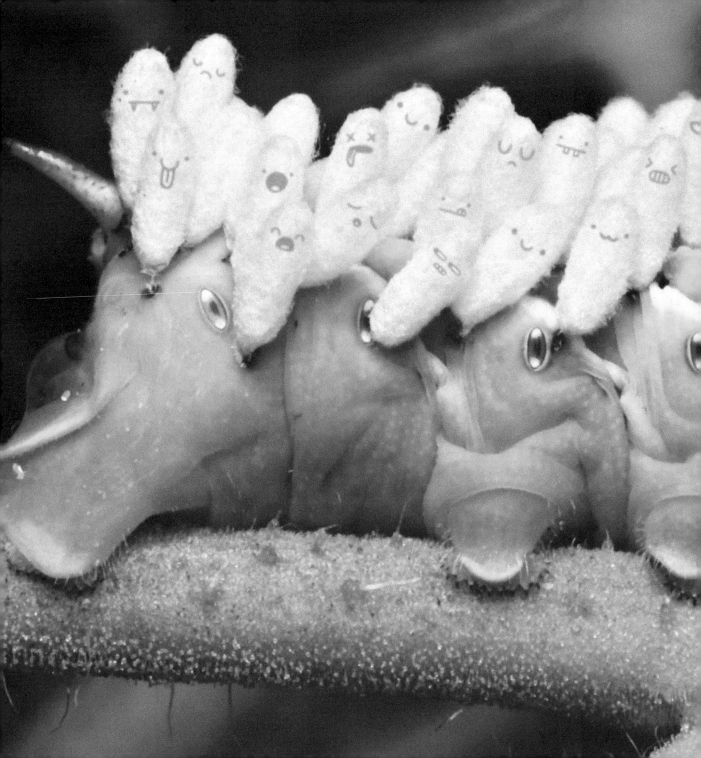

THANK YOU GOD
for animals on land
and sea that crawl...

Genesis 1: 20-25

THANK YOU GOD
for Adam and Eve that united
as one and was married.

Genesis 1: 20-25

THANK YOU GOD
for Sunday and all your
work was done. This
day is now a holy one.

Genesis 2: 1-3

THANK YOU GOD
for the Ten Commandments
to show each day. These
rules will show us the
right way.

Exodus 20:1-21

THANK YOU GOD
for your son. Jesus is a great gift for everyone.

Luke 1:31

GOD IS LOVE

and wants love to show, the love you have given me will always grow.

THANK YOU GOD!